THE CONFESSIONS OF A BLACK WOMAN

THE JOURNEY OF SELF-DISCOVERY AND EMPOWERMENT

Dr Lovella Mogere

Confessions of A Black Woman
Copyright © 2024 by Dr Lovella Mogere

All rights reserved. No part of this book may be reproduced or transmitted in any form or by any means without written permission from the author.

ISBN: 9798323530472

Printed in the USA by Nous Mass Media (www.nousmassmedia.com)

DEDICATION

To the resilient, powerful, and unyielding Black women whose stories have shaped the tapestry of our existence. You are the pillars of strength, the beacons of hope, and the embodiment of grace in the face of adversity. Your unwavering resilience, boundless love, and unwavering determination inspire us all to rise higher, reach further, and stand taller. This book is dedicated to you, with deepest admiration, respect, and love.

-Dr Lovella Mogere

DR LOVELLA MOGERE

TABLE OF CONTENTS

Foreword 6
Preface 8
Introduction 9
Chapter One 10
    The Mask: Hiding Behind Societal Expectations 10
    The Complexities of the Mask 11
    Confront The Mask That Shapes Our Identity 12
    Uncovering Moments of Liberation 13

Chapter Two 17
    Breaking Free: Embracing My True Identity 17
    The Voices of Doubt and Insecurity 18
    Breaking Free from the Constraints of the Mask 20

Chapter Three 22
    The Struggle: Navigating Racism and Discrimination ... 22
    The Multifaceted Layers of Adversity 23
    The Struggle 25

Chapter Four 26
    Finding My Voice: Overcoming Fear and Speaking Out ... 26
    How Do We Navigate The Complexities of Finding Our Voice? .. 27
    Uncover the Strength Within Ourselves 29

Chapter Five 31
    Healing Wounds: Confronting Trauma and Pain 31
    Intergenerational Trauma and Systemic Oppression 33
    The Stigma and Shame Surrounding Mental Illness 34

Chapter Six 38
    Rising Strong: Embracing Resilience and Inner Strength 38
    Challenges That Triumph Over Our Minds 39
    Nurturing Self-Gratitude and Appreciation 40

THE CONFESSIONS OF A BLACK WOMAN

Chapter Seven 43
   Embracing My Brilliance 43
   Confront What Comes To Undermine YOur Confidence 45
   Claim Your Power 47

Chapter Eight 50
   The Journey Ahead: Continuing To Grow and Thrive 50
   Embraced Your Power.. 51

Chapter Nine 54
   The Essence of You, Black Woman 54
   We Are the Architects of Our Own Destiny.................................. 55
   Black Women Carry Within Them the Legacy of Our Ancestors.. 57

Chapter Ten 60
   Honoring the Fortitude of The Black Women 60

Chapter Eleven 63
   Black Woman, You Are Enough 63

DR LOVELLA MOGERE

FOREWORD

In "Confessions of A Black Woman," we are invited into a sacred space where vulnerability meets strength, and authenticity reigns supreme. Through the lens of raw honesty and unfiltered storytelling, we embark on a journey into the heart and soul of Black womanhood—a journey filled with triumphs, challenges, joys, and sorrows.

As we turn the pages of this powerful book, we are reminded of the resilience, beauty, and power inherent in Black women everywhere. Each chapter shared within these pages is a testament to the depth of our experiences, the richness of our culture, and the strength of our spirit.

From the depths of pain to the heights of triumph, these chapters illuminate the complexities of our existence and celebrate the beauty of our diversity. They remind us of the importance of reclaiming our narratives, embracing our truths, and standing tall in our power.

"Confessions of A Black Woman" is more than just a collection of stories—it is a testament to the resilience, strength, and beauty of Black women everywhere. It is a reminder that our voices matter, our stories deserve to be heard, and our presence in this world is invaluable.

May this book serve as a source of inspiration, empowerment, and affirmation for Black women everywhere. May it remind us of our worth, our strength, and our limitless potential. And may it ignite a flame within each of us to continue shining brightly, unapologetically, and beautifully.

With deep appreciation and admiration,
#TheConfessionsOfABlackWomen

Hey Sis,

Expect to be profoundly impacted by Dr. Lovella Mogere as she takes you on a prolific excursion through "Confessions of A Black Woman". Upon reading this colossal composition, may your mind discover manifestation, your soul ascertain security, and your spirit experience solace in every aspect of YOU.

Through "The Confessions of a Black Woman", may you ascend and amplify your presence and voice throughout the earth as THE living epistle- read of all Black women!!

Your Sister,
Dr. Varenda S. Williams, Ph.D., D.D.
Author- "For Her Majesty's Eyes Only: Confessions Fit for the Marketplace Queen"

DR LOVELLA MOGERE

PREFACE

In the echoes of our shared experiences lies the essence of our collective journey. "Confessions of A Black Woman" is more than just a collection of stories—it is a testament to the resilience, strength, and beauty of Black women everywhere. As you turn the pages of this book, you will be invited into the intimate spaces of our lives, where vulnerability meets courage and authenticity reigns supreme.

In these pages, you will find unfiltered truths, raw emotions, and unapologetic reflections on the multifaceted experiences of being a Black woman in a world that often seeks to silence our voices and diminish our worth. Through these confessions, we reclaim our narratives, celebrate our heritage, and honor the legacies of those who came before us. Each chapter shared within these pages is a testament to the power of resilience, the beauty of diversity, and the importance of embracing our true selves. It is my hope that as you journey through these confessions, you will find solace, inspiration, and empowerment in knowing that you are not alone—that your story matters, and your voice deserves to be heard.

May this book serve as a beacon of light, illuminating the path toward self-discovery, healing, and unapologetic self-love. May it inspire you to embrace your truth, stand tall in your power, and forge ahead with unwavering determination. And may it remind you that within the depths of your soul lies the strength to overcome any obstacle and the resilience to rise, time and time again.

With love and solidarity,
Dr Lovella Mogere

INTRODUCTION

"Confessions of A Black Woman" is an unapologetically candid journey into the heart and soul of a woman navigating the complexities of her identity, heritage, and experiences. Through raw, poignant storytelling, this book delves deep into the joys, struggles, triumphs, and tribulations of being a Black woman in today's world. Prepare to be moved, inspired, and enlightened as you embark on this powerful exploration of self-discovery, resilience, and empowerment.

CHAPTER ONE

THE MASK: HIDING BEHIND SOCIETAL EXPECTATIONS

In the tapestry of our lives, Black women often find themselves weaving a delicate balance between authenticity and conformity—a balance that requires them to don a mask to navigate the expectations imposed upon them by society.

From a young age, Black women are taught to conform to narrow standards of beauty, behavior, and achievement. We are told to be strong, resilient, and unwavering in the face of adversity, even when our souls cry out for solace and support. We are expected to embody the myth of the "Strong Black Woman," a stereotype that robs us of our humanity and denies us the space to express vulnerability or seek help.

The mask we wear is a shield, a barrier between our true selves and the outside world. Behind its carefully crafted facade, *we hide our fears, insecurities, and doubts, presenting a version of ourselves that is palatable to others but often feels foreign to our own hearts.* But what is the cost of wearing this mask? What toll does it take on our mental, emotional, and spiritual well-being? And how do we reclaim our authenticity in a world that seeks to diminish our voices and erase our truths?

In this chapter, we will explore the complexities of the mask—the layers of expectations, stereotypes, and pressures that Black women must navigate on a daily basis. We will confront the ways in which the mask shapes our identities, relationships, and sense of self-worth, and the ways in which it limits our ability to fully embrace humanity.

But we will also **uncover moments of liberation**—moments when we dare to remove the mask and reveal our true selves to the world. *We will celebrate the power of vulnerability, the beauty of imperfection, and the strength that comes from embracing our authentic selves.*

As we journey through this chapter, let us remember that the mask is *not our identity—it is a construct imposed upon us by society, and one that we have the power to shed.* Let us honor our truths, embrace our flaws, and stand boldly in our authenticity, knowing that our voices are worthy of being heard, and our stories are worthy of being told.

THE COMPLEXITIES OF THE MASK

The complexities of the mask lie in its ability to **conceal our true selves** while simultaneously shaping our interactions, perceptions, and experiences in the world. Behind the mask, we **hide our vulnerabilities**, fears, and insecurities, presenting a facade of strength and resilience to the outside world. Yet, this facade often comes at a cost, as we navigate the pressure to conform to societal expectations and stereotypes.

The mask is a product of societal conditioning—a response to the narrow standards of beauty, behavior, and achievement imposed upon us from a young age. It compels us to mold ourselves into predetermined roles and personas, denying us the space to express our authentic thoughts, emotions, and desires. At the same time, the *mask serves as a shield, protecting us from the judgment, discrimination, and prejudice that we may face as Black women in society.* It allows us to **navigate spaces that may not always be safe or welcoming, providing us with a sense of security and control in an often-hostile world.**

Yet, behind the *mask lies a sense of dissonance—a feeling of disconnect between our true selves and the personas we present to others.* We may struggle to reconcile the expectations placed upon us with our own desires and aspirations, grappling with feelings of inadequacy, impostor syndrome, and self-doubt.

Despite these challenges, *the mask also offers moments of empowerment and resilience.* **It allows us to adapt, navigate, and survive in environments that may seek to diminish our voices and erase our truths.** It serves as a testament to our strength, resilience, and ability to thrive in the face of adversity.

Ultimately, the complexities of the mask remind us of the multifaceted nature of our identities as Black women. *It is a symbol of the contradictions, challenges, and triumphs that shape our lived experiences, and a reminder of the power that lies in embracing our authenticity and reclaiming our truths.*

CONFRONT THE MASK THAT SHAPES OUR IDENTITY

Confronting the ways in which the mask shapes our identities requires a deep and introspective journey into our thoughts, feelings, and experiences. Here are some steps to help navigate this process:

1. **Self-Reflection:** Take time to reflect on your thoughts, emotions, and behaviors, and consider how they may be influenced by societal expectations and stereotypes. Ask yourself questions such as: What masks do I wear in different areas of my life? How do these masks impact my sense of self-worth and identity?
2. **Identify Patterns**: Pay attention to recurring patterns or themes in your life, particularly those related to conformity, people-pleasing, or self-censorship. Notice when you feel pressure to conform to societal expectations or suppress aspects of your identity to fit in.
3. **Challenge Assumptions:** Question the assumptions and beliefs that underlie the masks you wear. Are these beliefs based on truth and authenticity, or are they influenced by external

pressures and expectations? Challenge yourself to think critically about the narratives you've internalized about what it means to be a Black woman in society.
4. **Seek Support:** Reach out to trusted friends, family members, or mentors who can provide support and guidance as you navigate this process of self-exploration. Having a supportive community can help validate your experiences and provide perspective as you confront the ways in which the mask shapes your identity.
5. **Practice Self-Compassion:** Be gentle and compassionate with yourself as you uncover the layers of your identity and confront the masks you've worn. Recognize that this process may be challenging and uncomfortable at times, but it is an essential step towards greater self-awareness and authenticity.
6. **Embrace Authenticity:** Finally, commit to embracing your authentic self and reclaiming your truth. Celebrate the unique qualities, strengths, and vulnerabilities that make you who you are, and honor the complexity and richness of your identity as a Black woman. Remember that true liberation comes from embracing and celebrating your authentic self, free from the constraints of societal expectations and stereotypes.

UNCOVERING MOMENTS OF LIBERATION

Uncovering moments of liberation, where we dare to remove the mask and reveal our true selves to the world, involves a deeply personal and transformative journey of self-discovery and self-acceptance. Here are some ways we can uncover and embrace these moments:

1. **Self-Reflection:** Take time to reflect on your experiences, thoughts, and feelings, and identify moments when you have felt most authentic and true to yourself. Consider the circumstances and environments that allowed you to remove the mask and express your identity freely.

2. **Courageous Vulnerability:** Embrace vulnerability as a source of strength and authenticity. Recognize that removing the mask requires courage and resilience, as it involves risking rejection or judgment from others. However, it is often through moments of vulnerability that we experience the deepest connections and most profound sense of liberation.
3. **Authentic Expression:** Explore different forms of self-expression that feel authentic to you, whether through art, writing, music, or movement. Engaging in creative practices can provide a powerful outlet for expressing your true self and connecting with others who resonate with your authenticity.
4. **Supportive Relationships:** Surround yourself with supportive and accepting individuals who encourage you to be your true self. Cultivate relationships with people who celebrate your uniqueness and affirm your worth, allowing you to feel safe and empowered to remove the mask in their presence.
5. **Mindfulness and Presence:** Practice mindfulness and presence as a way of cultivating self-awareness and reconnecting with your innermost truths. By staying grounded in the present moment and tuning into your thoughts and feelings, you can more easily recognize when you are wearing the mask and take steps to remove it.
6. **Celebrate Small Victories:** Acknowledge and celebrate small victories along the journey towards authenticity. Whether it's speaking your truth in a challenging situation or expressing yourself authentically in a new context, each moment of liberation is a step towards greater self-acceptance and empowerment.
7. **Embrace Imperfection:** Embrace the imperfection and messiness of the journey towards authenticity. Recognize that it's okay to stumble or falter along the way, and that growth often comes from embracing our vulnerabilities and learning from our experiences.

THE CONFESSIONS OF A BLACK WOMAN

Uncovering moments of liberation is about embracing the fullness of who you are and allowing yourself to be seen and heard in all your complexity and beauty. It's a courageous act of self-love and self-acceptance that opens the door to deeper connections, greater fulfillment, and profound personal growth.

The cost of wearing the mask is multifaceted, taking a toll on our mental, emotional, and spiritual well-being in profound ways. Mentally, the constant pressure to conform to societal expectations and suppress our true selves can lead to feelings of anxiety, depression, and disconnection from our authentic identity.

Emotionally, wearing the mask may result in a sense of internal conflict, as we grapple with the dissonance between who we are and who we feel compelled to be. Spiritually, the mask can hinder our ability to connect with our innermost truths and live in alignment with our values and beliefs.

To reclaim our authenticity in a world that seeks to diminish our voices and erase our truths, we must first recognize the power of our own agency and voice. By acknowledging the ways in which the mask has shaped our identities and impacted our well-being, we can begin the process of dismantling its influence and reclaiming our true selves. This may involve setting boundaries, challenging societal norms, and practicing radical self-acceptance and self-love.

Additionally, finding community and solidarity with other Black women who share similar experiences can provide validation, support, and collective strength in the journey towards authenticity. By uplifting each other's voices and amplifying our truths, we can create spaces of empowerment and liberation where our identities are celebrated and honored.

Reclaiming our authenticity requires courage, resilience, and a commitment to living in alignment with our deepest truths. It is an ongoing process of self-discovery and self-affirmation, but one that is essential for our mental, emotional, and spiritual well-being. By embracing our authentic selves and refusing to be defined by society's narrow expectations, we can forge a path towards greater wholeness, fulfillment, and liberation.

CHAPTER TWO

BREAKING FREE: EMBRACING MY TRUE IDENTITY

In the journey towards authenticity, there comes a pivotal moment when the weight of societal expectations becomes unbearable, and the desire to break free from the confines of the mask grows stronger than ever. This is the moment when we must summon the courage to confront our fears, embrace our identity, and step boldly into the light of our authenticity. For too long, I had allowed myself to be shaped and defined by the expectations of others, conforming to societal norms, and wearing the mask of acceptability to fit in. But deep within me, there was a yearning for something more—a longing to peel back the layers of pretense and reveal the essence of who I truly was.

The journey of *breaking free began with a moment of radical self-honesty—a moment of looking in the mirror and acknowledging the disconnect between the image I projected onto the world and the truth that lay hidden beneath the surface.* It was a moment of reckoning, a moment of recognizing that I could no longer live a life that was not aligned with my authentic self. With this realization came a sense of liberation—a sense of empowerment that fueled my determination to **shed the layers** of the mask and embrace my identity, unapologetically and without reservation. It was a process of **rediscovering myself**, reclaiming lost parts of my soul, and embracing the fullness of who I was meant to be.

Breaking free meant confronting the voices of doubt and insecurity that whispered in the shadows of my mind, telling me that I was not enough, that I did not belong. It meant challenging the internalized beliefs and limiting narratives that had kept me small and silent for far too long. But as I began to peel back the layers of the mask, I discovered a reservoir of strength and resilience within me—a strength born of adversity and nurtured by the fire of my own determination. With each layer that fell away, I felt lighter, more alive, more authentically myself.

Embracing my true identity was not *without its challenges.* There were moments of doubt and uncertainty, moments when I questioned whether I had the courage to continue this path. But with each step forward, I found myself surrounded by a community of fellow travelers—others who, like me, were breaking free from the constraints of the mask and embracing their true selves.

Together, we lifted each other up, offering support, encouragement, and unwavering belief in the power of authenticity. And as we stood shoulder to shoulder, united in our quest for liberation, we became living testament to the transformative power of embracing our true identity.

THE VOICES OF DOUBT AND INSECURITY

Confronting the voices of doubt and insecurity can be a challenging but empowering process. Here are some strategies to help you confront and overcome these inner obstacles:

1. **Recognize and Acknowledge the Voices:** Start by becoming aware of the negative thoughts and beliefs that contribute to your feelings of doubt and insecurity. Take note of the specific thoughts or inner dialogues that arise when you face challenges or setbacks.
2. **Challenge Negative Thoughts:** Once you've identified the negative thoughts, challenge them with rational and evidence-based reasoning. Ask yourself if there is any concrete evidence to support these thoughts, or if they are simply based on fear or past experiences. Replace negative self-talk with positive

affirmations and statements that affirm your worth and capabilities.
3. **Practice Self-Compassion:** Treat yourself with kindness and compassion, especially when you're feeling doubtful or insecure. Acknowledge that it's normal to experience self-doubt at times and remind yourself that you are worthy of love and acceptance just as you are.
4. **Focus on Your Strengths:** Shift your focus away from your perceived weaknesses and shortcomings, and instead focus on your strengths and accomplishments. Make a list of your achievements, talents, and qualities that you admire about yourself, and refer to it whenever you need a confidence boost.
5. **Set Realistic Goals:** Break down your goals into smaller, manageable tasks, and celebrate your progress along the way. Setting realistic and achievable goals can help build confidence and provide a sense of accomplishment, which can in turn help combat feelings of doubt and insecurity.
6. **Seek Support:** Reach out to friends, family members, or a trusted mentor for support and encouragement. Talking to someone who understands and validates your feelings can provide perspective and reassurance during times of doubt.
7. **Practice Mindfulness:** Engage in mindfulness practices such as meditation, deep breathing, or yoga to help calm your mind and bring awareness to the present moment. Mindfulness can help you observe your thoughts and emotions without judgment, allowing you to respond to them in a more constructive way.
8. **Take Action Despite Fear:** Remember that courage is not the absence of fear, but the willingness to take action in spite of it. Instead of waiting until you feel completely confident, take small steps towards your goals even if you feel afraid or uncertain. Each step forward will help build momentum and confidence over time.

By implementing these strategies, you can confront the voices of doubt and insecurity with courage and resilience, and ultimately cultivate a greater sense of self-confidence and self-assurance.

BREAKING FREE FROM THE CONSTRAINTS OF THE MASK

Breaking free from the constraints of the mask is a *transformative journey that requires courage*, self-awareness, and a willingness to embrace vulnerability. Here are some steps to help you begin this empowering process:

1. **Acknowledge the Mask:** Start by recognizing the ways in which you have been hiding behind the mask. Reflect on the roles you play, the personas you adopt, and the behaviors you engage in to conform to societal expectations or protect yourself from judgment or rejection.
2. **Explore Your Authentic Self:** Take time to connect with your true self beneath the layers of the mask. Engage in self-reflection, journaling, or creative expression to explore your values, beliefs, passions, and desires. Identify the aspects of yourself that you have been suppressing or denying in order to fit in or avoid discomfort.
3. **Challenge Limiting Beliefs:** Identify the limiting beliefs or negative self-talk that have kept you trapped in the mask. Question the validity of these beliefs and consider how they may be holding you back from living authentically. Replace self-doubt with self-compassion and cultivate a mindset of growth and possibility.
4. **Practice Vulnerability:** Embrace vulnerability as a strength rather than a weakness. Allow yourself to be seen and heard authentically, even if it feels uncomfortable or risky. Share your

thoughts, feelings, and experiences with trusted friends or loved ones who can offer support and validation.
5. **Set Boundaries:** Establish healthy boundaries to protect your authentic self from external pressures, expectations, or judgments. Learn to say no to activities, relationships, or commitments that compromise your values or integrity. Prioritize self-care and prioritize your own needs and well-being.
6. **Take Small Steps:** Break free from the mask gradually by taking small steps outside your comfort zone. Experiment with expressing your true thoughts, feelings, and preferences in low-risk situations. Celebrate your courage and resilience as you navigate the challenges of authenticity.
7. **Seek Support:** Surround yourself with people who accept and appreciate you for who you truly are. Seek out communities, groups, or mentors who share your values and support your journey toward authenticity. Remember that you are not alone in this process, and that seeking support is a sign of strength, not weakness.
8. **Celebrate Your Uniqueness:** Embrace your uniqueness and celebrate the qualities that make you who you are. Recognize that authenticity is not about conforming to a standard or fitting into a mold, but about embracing your individuality and honoring your truth. Allow yourself to shine brightly and authentically in the world.

By breaking free from the constraints of the mask, you can cultivate a deeper sense of self-awareness, self-acceptance, and self-expression. *Embrace the journey of authenticity* with courage and compassion, knowing that the freedom to be yourself is the greatest gift you can give yourself.

CHAPTER THREE

THE STRUGGLE: NAVIGATING RACISM AND DISCRIMINATION

In this chapter, we **confront** the harsh realities of racism and discrimination that permeate every aspect of Black women's lives. We delve into the *systemic injustices, microaggressions*, and overt acts of racism that Black women face daily, both in their personal and professional spheres. Through candid narratives and poignant reflections, we explore the toll that racism takes on our mental health, emotional well-being, and sense of self-worth. We examine the ways in which these experiences of marginalization and oppression intersect with other aspects of our identities, such as gender, sexuality, and class.

We confront the *pervasive stereotypes* and tropes that perpetuate *harmful narratives* about Black women, from the **hypersexualized Jezebel to the angry Black woman**. We challenge these narratives and reclaim our humanity, asserting our right to exist unapologetically in a world that often seeks to erase us. But amidst the struggle, we find resilience. We uncover moments of strength, solidarity, and resistance, as Black women come together to support one another, uplift one another, and fight for justice. We celebrate the beauty, brilliance, and resilience of Black womanhood, even in the face of adversity.

As we navigate the complexities of racism and discrimination, we are reminded of the importance of community, allyship, and self-care. We find *solace in the bonds of sisterhood, the power of our voices*, and the resilience of our spirits.

THE CONFESSIONS OF A BLACK WOMAN

In the pages that follow, we will continue to explore the multifaceted experiences of Black womanhood, shining a light on the struggles, triumphs, joys, and sorrows that shape our lives. But as we do, let us remember that our voices matter, our stories deserve to be heard, and our existence is resistance. The Struggle: Navigating Racism and Discrimination." May this chapter serve as a testament to our resilience, our strength, and our unwavering commitment to justice and liberation.

THE MULTIFACETED LAYERS OF ADVERSITY

In the journey of life, the path of a Black woman is often fraught with the daunting challenge of navigating through the intricate web of racism and discrimination. The intricate nuances of these struggles, illuminating the multifaceted layers of adversity faced by Black women in a society rife with systemic biases and prejudices.

1. **Unveiling the Veil of Stereotypes:** From the persistent portrayal of the "angry Black woman" trope to the fetishization of Black bodies, Black women grapple with the burden of enduring harmful stereotypes that undermine their humanity and diminish their individuality. These stereotypes not only perpetuate damaging narratives but also serve as barriers to genuine connection and understanding.
2. **Microaggressions: The Sting of Subtlety:** Microaggressions, those insidious yet potent slights and comments, punctuate the everyday experiences of Black women. Whether it's the suspicious glances received while shopping or the condescending remarks questioning their competence in professional spheres, these microaggressions chip away at their sense of self-worth and belonging.
3. **Systemic Shackles: Institutionalized Racism:** The pervasive specter of systemic racism infiltrates various facets of society,

4. manifesting in the form of barriers to education, employment, healthcare, and justice. Black women find themselves ensnared at the crossroads of intersecting oppressions, grappling with impediments that hinder their pursuit of advancement and equitable treatment.
5. **The Emotional Burden:** Navigating the treacherous terrain of racism and discrimination exacts a profound emotional toll on Black women. The incessant pressure to prove their worth, the looming specter of racial profiling, and the relentless struggle against marginalization sow seeds of anger, sorrow, and weariness within their hearts.
6. **Intersectionality at Play:** Black women occupy a unique intersection of race and gender, confronting challenges that diverge from those encountered by Black men or White women. The complexities of intersectionality magnify the layers of discrimination faced by Black women, necessitating a nuanced understanding of their lived experiences. Black women occupy a unique intersection of race and gender, confronting challenges that diverge from those encountered by Black men or White women. The complexities of intersectionality magnify the layers of discrimination faced by Black women, necessitating a nuanced understanding of their lived experiences.
7. **Resilience Amidst Adversity:** Despite the formidable challenges they confront, Black women exhibit unparalleled resilience and fortitude in the face of adversity. Drawing strength from communal support, cultural heritage, and unwavering self-assurance, Black women cultivate coping mechanisms that empower them to persevere and prosper amidst adversity.
8. **A Call to Action:** In the crucible of adversity, Black women emerge as stalwart advocates for change, spearheading movements for racial justice and equality. Through grassroots mobilization, political activism, and narrative amplification,

Black women galvanize efforts to dismantle oppressive structures and foster a more inclusive and equitable society.

We will continue to **confront** the harsh realities of racism and discrimination while **celebrating** the indomitable spirit, resilience, and brilliance of Black women. By shedding light on these struggles, we endeavor to foster empathy, ignite dialogue, and inspire collective action in the ongoing pursuit of liberation and justice for all.

THE STRUGGLE

Navigating Racism and Discrimination" serves as a poignant testament to the resilience and perseverance of Black women in the face of systemic injustices. Through the exploration of stereotypes, microaggressions, systemic barriers, emotional burdens, and the intersectionality of oppression, this chapter sheds light on the multifaceted nature of the challenges faced by Black women. Yet, amidst the darkness of adversity, there shines a beacon of hope and resilience. Black women, buoyed by their unwavering strength and collective solidarity, continue to defy the odds and push boundaries in the relentless pursuit of justice and equality. **Their voices, though often marginalized and silenced, reverberate with a resounding call for change and transformation.**

As we reflect on the struggles outlined in this chapter, let us heed the call to action and stand in solidarity with Black women in the fight against racism and discrimination. Let us amplify their voices, uplift their stories, and work tirelessly to dismantle the oppressive structures that perpetuate inequality and injustice. In *honoring the fortitude of Black women*, we move closer towards the realization of a more just, equitable, and inclusive society for all. Let us continue to stand united in the pursuit of a brighter future, where every *Black woman can thrive, flourish, and shine without fear or hindrance.*

CHAPTER FOUR

FINDING MY VOICE: OVERCOMING FEAR AND SPEAKING OUT

In this chapter, we embark on a journey of *self-discovery and empowerment* as we confront the fear and uncertainty that often accompanies finding our voice in a world that seeks to silence us. We delve into the challenges and obstacles that stand in our way, and the courage and resilience it takes to overcome them.

Through *personal anecdotes*, reflections, and insights, we explore the ways in which fear manifests in our lives, holding us back from expressing our truths and standing up for what we believe in. We *confront the internalized messages* of doubt and insecurity that whisper in our ears, telling us that our voices don't matter, that our stories aren't important. But amidst the fear, we find courage. We *uncover* the strength within ourselves to speak out, to raise our voices, and to demand to be heard. We share stories of triumph and resilience, of overcoming adversity and finding power in our vulnerability.

As we navigate the complexities of finding our voice, we discover the importance of self-love, self-acceptance, and self-compassion. We learn to embrace our imperfections, celebrate our unique perspectives, and stand confidently in our truths. Through the process of finding our voice, we not only empower ourselves but also inspire others to do the same. We become beacons of hope and agents of change, shining brightly in a world that desperately needs our light.

In the chapters that follow, we will continue to explore the journey of finding our voice, shining a light on the challenges, triumphs, and transformations that shape our paths. But as we do, let us remember that our voices have the power to change the world—to spark conversations, ignite movements, and create lasting change.

Welcome to Chapter 4 of "Confessions of a Black Woman: Finding My Voice: Overcoming Fear and Speaking Out." May this chapter serve as a source of inspiration, empowerment, and affirmation as we continue to raise our voices and claim our rightful place in the world.

HOW DO WE NAVIGATE THE COMPLEXITIES OF FINDING OUR VOICE?

Navigating the complexities of finding our voice is a deeply personal journey that requires self-awareness, courage, and perseverance. Here are some steps to help navigate this journey:

1. **Self-Reflection:** Take time to reflect on your experiences, values, and beliefs. Explore what matters most to you and what you're passionate about. This self-reflection can help you better understand yourself and your authentic voice.
2. **Identify Barriers:** Identify any internal or external barriers that may be holding you back from expressing your voice. These barriers could include self-doubt, fear of judgment, or lack of confidence. By recognizing these obstacles, you can begin to address and overcome them.
3. **Practice Self-Compassion:** Be kind and compassionate with yourself as you navigate this process. Understand that finding your voice is a journey, and it's okay to encounter setbacks along the way. Treat yourself with the same kindness and understanding that you would offer to a friend.
4. **Speak Your Truth:** Start by speaking your truth in small, safe spaces. Share your thoughts, feelings, and opinions with trusted

friends, family members, or mentors who will support and encourage you. As you gain confidence, gradually expand your circle, and share your voice more widely.

5. **Honor Your Values:** Stay true to your values and beliefs as you find your voice. Let them guide you in expressing yourself authentically and standing up for what you believe in. When your actions align with your values, you'll feel more grounded and confident in your voice.

6. **Seek Feedback:** Seek feedback from others on your communication style and the impact of your voice. Listen openly to their perspectives and use their feedback to refine and strengthen your voice. However, remember that ultimately, your voice is yours alone, and you have the final say in how you express yourself.

7. **Embrace Vulnerability:** Embrace vulnerability as a source of strength and authenticity. Allow yourself to be open and honest, even when it feels uncomfortable or scary. Vulnerability fosters connection and allows others to see the real you behind your words.

8. **Practice Assertiveness:** Practice assertiveness in your interactions with others. Assertiveness involves expressing your thoughts, feelings, and needs clearly and respectfully, while also listening to and respecting the perspectives of others. Assertive communication can help you assert your voice with confidence and clarity.

9. **Celebrate Your Progress:** Celebrate each step forward in finding your voice, no matter how small. Acknowledge your courage and resilience and celebrate the progress you've made on your journey. Remember that finding your voice is a lifelong process, and every step counts.

By following these steps and staying true to yourself, you can navigate the complexities of finding your voice and express yourself authentically and confidently in the world.

UNCOVER THE STRENGTH WITHIN OURSELVES

Uncovering the strength within ourselves is a transformative journey of self-discovery and empowerment, where we embrace our inner resilience and courage to navigate life's challenges and fulfill our true potential. It involves:

1. **Self-Reflection:** Take time to reflect on your experiences, challenges, and achievements. Recognize the resilience and determination you've shown in overcoming obstacles.
2. **Identifying Inner Resources:** Explore your inner resources, such as courage, resilience, and perseverance. Acknowledge the times when you've demonstrated these qualities in the face of adversity.
3. **Facing Challenges**: Embrace challenges as opportunities for growth and learning. Trust in your ability to overcome obstacles and navigate difficult situations with grace and determination.
4. **Cultivating Self-**Belief: Cultivate a strong belief in yourself and your capabilities. Remind yourself of your strength and accomplishments, and trust in your capacity to overcome challenges.
5. **Seeking Support:** Reach out to friends, family, or mentors for support and encouragement. Surround yourself with positive influences that uplift and inspire you on your journey.
6. **Setting Goals:** Set meaningful goals that align with your values and aspirations. Brak them down into manageable steps and take consistent action towards achieving them.

7. **Practicing Self-Care**: Prioritize self-care and nourish your mind, body, and spirit. Take time to rest, recharge, and engage in activities that bring you joy and fulfillment.

8. **Embracing Vulnerability**: Embrace vulnerability as a sign of strength and authenticity. Allow yourself to be open and vulnerable, knowing that it is through vulnerability that we connect with ourselves and others on a deeper level.

By uncovering the strength within us, we tap into our inner reservoir of courage, and determination, empowering us to navigate life's challenges with confidence and grace. *Let us remember that the journey to authenticity and integrity is not always easy*, but it is deeply rewarding. As we navigate the complexities of life, let us uncover the strength within ourselves to embrace our true selves and live with integrity.

Integrity guides our actions, ensuring that we remain true to ourselves and our principles, even in the face of temptation or hardship. It is the bedrock of trust, respect, and ethical conduct, fostering genuine connections and meaningful relationships.

May we draw upon this inner strength to navigate life's challenges with grace, resilience, and courage. And may we inspire others to do the same, creating a world where authenticity and integrity are celebrated and cherished. In uncovering the strength within us, we discover our true power—the power to shape our destinies, create positive change, and leave a lasting impact on the world.

So let us embrace our inner strength wholeheartedly, knowing that it is the key to unlocking our fullest potential and living a life of purpose, passion, and fulfillment.

CHAPTER FIVE

HEALING WOUNDS: CONFRONTING TRAUMA AND PAIN

In this chapter, we delve into the courageous journey of **confronting trauma and pain** to facilitate healing and growth. Trauma manifests in various forms, from *childhood experiences to adulthood challenges*, and its *effects can linger, impacting our emotional, mental, and physical well-being*. We explore the importance of acknowledging and validating our pain, understanding its roots, and seeking support and resources for healing. Through introspection, therapy, and self-care practices, we embark on a transformative path toward healing, reclaiming our power, and embracing a future defined by resilience and wholeness.

We will *delve into the wounds* that have been inflicted upon us—physical, emotional, and spiritual—and explore the process of healing and finding peace.

Through raw and honest narratives, we courageously *confront the traumas of our past and the scars they have left behind*. We share stories of resilience and survival, of navigating the darkest corners of our minds and emerging stronger on the other side.

We **explore the impact of intergenerational trauma and systemic oppression** on our *mental health and well-being*, recognizing the ways in which our *histories shape our present realities*. We **confront the stigma** and shame *surrounding mental illness* within our communities and advocate for greater awareness and support.

As we *journey through the process of healing, we embrace practices of self-care, self-compassion, and self-love.* We prioritize our mental health and well-being, seeking out therapy, support groups, and holistic healing modalities to nurture our souls and soothe our spirits.

But healing is not a linear journey—it is messy, nonlinear, and often painful. We *confront setbacks, relapses, and triggers* along the way, but we also *celebrate moments of breakthrough, growth, and transformation.*

In the midst of our healing journey, we **discover** *the power of community and connection.* We lean on one another for support, compassion, and understanding, knowing that we are not alone in our struggles.

Through the process of *healing our own wounds*, we also become healers for others, offering empathy, compassion, and solidarity to those who are still on their own healing journey.

In the pages that follow, we will continue to explore the process of healing wounds, shining a light on the challenges, triumphs, and transformations that shape our paths. But as we do, let us remember that healing is possible, and that we are worthy of love, support, and healing.

Welcome to Chapter 5 of "Confessions of a Black Woman: Healing Wounds: Confronting Trauma and Pain." May this chapter serve as a source of comfort, inspiration, and empowerment as we continue to navigate the complexities of healing and reclaiming our wholeness.

INTERGENERATIONAL TRAUMA AND SYSTEMIC OPPRESSION

The impact of intergenerational trauma and systemic oppression is profound and far-reaching, spanning generations and permeating every aspect of individuals' lives and communities. *Intergenerational trauma refers to the transmission of trauma from one generation to the next, often manifesting as unresolved pain, grief, and suffering that is passed down through family systems.* This **trauma** can stem from **historical events such as slavery, colonization, genocide, and racial violence, as well as ongoing experiences of discrimination, poverty, and marginalization.**

Systemic oppression, on the other hand, refers to the *structural barriers and injustices embedded within social, political, and economic systems that perpetuate inequality and discrimination against marginalized groups.* These **systems of oppression**—such as *racism, sexism, homophobia, ableism, and classism*—create and maintain power imbalances that disadvantage certain groups while privileging others.

The combined impact of intergenerational trauma and systemic oppression can have devastating effects on individuals' *mental, emotional, and physical well-being*. It can lead to *chronic stress, anxiety, depression, post-traumatic stress disorder* (**PTSD**), substance abuse, and other mental health issues. It can also contribute to physical health disparities, including higher rates of chronic diseases such as diabetes, hypertension, and heart disease.

Furthermore, intergenerational trauma and systemic oppression can affect *individuals' sense of identity, self-worth, and belonging.* It can erode trust in institutions and communities, perpetuate cycles of poverty and violence, and limit opportunities for social and economic advancement. It can also impact relationships, parenting practices, and family dynamics, creating patterns of dysfunction and disconnection.

Addressing the impact of intergenerational trauma and systemic oppression requires a *multifaceted approach that acknowledges the historical roots of trauma and oppression* while also addressing present-day **inequities and injustices**. This includes providing culturally competent mental health services, promoting *healing-centered approaches* to **trauma recovery**, **advocating for policies that dismantle systemic barriers and promote equity and inclusion**, and *fostering community resilience and empowerment*. It also involves amplifying the voices and experiences of those most affected by trauma and oppression and working collaboratively to create a more just and compassionate society for future generations.

THE STIGMA AND SHAME SURROUNDING MENTAL ILLNESS

Confronting the stigma and shame surrounding mental illness requires a *concerted effort at both individual and societal levels*. Here are some steps that can be taken:

1. **Education and Awareness:** Increasing public education and awareness about mental health conditions is essential for challenging stigma and misinformation. This includes providing accurate information about the causes, symptoms, and treatment of mental illnesses, as well as debunking common myths and misconceptions.
2. **Open Dialogue:** Encouraging open and honest conversations about mental health can help reduce stigma and create a supportive environment for those struggling with mental illness. This involves breaking down barriers to communication and

creating spaces where people feel comfortable sharing their experiences without fear of judgment or discrimination.
3. **Challenging Stereotypes:** Challenging stereotypes and negative portrayals of mental illness in the media and popular culture can help combat stigma and promote understanding and empathy. This includes advocating for more accurate and compassionate depictions of mental health issues in movies, TV shows, and other forms of media.
4. **Language Matters:** Using respectful and non-stigmatizing language when talking about mental health is important for promoting dignity and respect for individuals living with mental illness. This includes avoiding derogatory terms and labels, such as "crazy" or "psycho," and instead using person-first language that emphasizes the individual rather than their diagnosis.
5. **Empathy and Support:** Showing empathy and support for individuals struggling with mental illness can go a long way in reducing stigma and promoting healing. This involves listening without judgment, offering validation and encouragement, and providing practical support and resources when needed.
6. **Advocacy and Policy Change:** Advocating for policies and initiatives that promote mental health awareness, access to treatment, and social inclusion is essential for addressing systemic barriers and discrimination. This includes advocating for mental health parity laws, anti-discrimination policies, and increased funding for mental health services and support.
7. **Role Modeling:** Being open about one's own experiences with mental health challenges can help reduce stigma and inspire others to seek help and support. By sharing personal stories of resilience and recovery, individuals can show that mental illness is not a sign of weakness or failure, but rather a common human experience that can be overcome with the right support and resources.

Confronting the stigma and shame surrounding mental illness requires a *collective effort that involves raising awareness, challenging stereotypes, promoting empathy and support, advocating for policy change, and fostering a culture of acceptance and inclusion for all individuals, regardless of their mental health status.*

In the "Healing Wounds: Confronting Trauma and Pain," we recognize that the journey of healing is not a solitary path but a collective endeavor—one that requires courage, vulnerability, and compassion. Throughout this chapter, we have delved into the depths of our pain, confronted the traumas of our past, and embarked on a transformative journey toward healing and wholeness.

We have explored the profound impact of intergenerational trauma and systemic oppression on our mental, emotional, and physical well-being, acknowledging the deep-seated wounds that have been passed down through generations. We have confronted the stigma and shame surrounding mental illness within our communities, advocating for greater awareness, understanding, and support.

In the midst of our healing journey, we have embraced practices of self-care, self-compassion, and self-love, prioritizing our mental health and well-being as we navigate the complexities of recovery. We have celebrated moments of breakthrough, growth, and transformation, recognizing that healing is not a linear process, but a messy, nonlinear journey filled with setbacks and triumphs. As we continue to navigate the complexities of healing and reclaiming our wholeness, let us remember that we are not alone in our struggles. We lean on one another for support, compassion, and understanding, knowing that together, we can overcome even the darkest of times.

In the pages that follow, we will delve into the journey of healing wounds, shining a light on the challenges, triumphs, and transformations that shape our paths. But as we do, let us hold onto the knowledge that healing is possible, and that we are worthy of love, support, and healing.

May this chapter serve as a source of comfort, inspiration, and empowerment as we continue to confront our traumas, embrace our vulnerabilities, and reclaim our power. Together, we will journey toward a future defined by resilience, wholeness, and hope.

CHAPTER SIX

RISING STRONG: EMBRACING RESILIENCE AND INNER STRENGTH

As we navigate the trials and tribulations of life, we learn to lean into our vulnerability, embracing it as a source of strength rather than weakness. We recognize that it is through our struggles that we grow, evolve, and ultimately become the people we are meant to be.

But resilience is not just about bouncing back from adversity—it's also about finding meaning and purpose in our pain. We discover the transformative power of storytelling, as we share our experiences with others and find connection and healing in the process.

Through the process of rising strong, we cultivate a deep sense of gratitude and appreciation for the beauty and resilience of the human spirit. We recognize that our struggles do not define us—they empower us to become our most authentic, empowered selves.

In the pages that follow, we will continue to explore the journey of rising strong, shining a light on the challenges, triumphs, and transformations that shape our paths. But as we do, let us remember that we are resilient, we are strong, and we have the power to overcome anything life throws our way.

Welcome to Chapter 6 of "Confessions of a Black Woman: Rising Strong: Embracing Resilience and Inner Strength." May this chapter serve as a reminder of the strength that lies within you, and may it inspire you to rise stronger than ever before.

CHALLENGES THAT TRIUMPH OVER OUR MINDS

Confronting the challenges that triumph over our minds requires resilience, self-awareness, and proactive strategies. Here are steps to help navigate and overcome these obstacles:

1. **Identify the Challenges:** Begin by recognizing the specific challenges that are affecting your mental well-being. This could include self-doubt, negative thought patterns, fear of failure, or anxiety about the future.
2. **Practice Self-Awareness:** Cultivate mindfulness and self-awareness to observe your thoughts and emotions without judgment. Pay attention to how these challenges manifest in your mind and body.
3. **Challenge Negative Thoughts:** When negative thoughts arise, challenge them with evidence-based reasoning and positive affirmations. Replace self-limiting beliefs with empowering statements that affirm your worth and capabilities.
4. **Develop Coping Strategies**: Build a toolbox of coping strategies to manage stress and overwhelm. This could include deep breathing exercises, progressive muscle relaxation, visualization techniques, or mindfulness meditation.
5. **Set Realistic Goals:** Break down larger goals into smaller, achievable steps to prevent feeling overwhelmed. Celebrate each milestone along the way, recognizing your progress and resilience.
6. Seek Support: Don't hesitate to reach out to friends, family, or a therapist for support and guidance. Talking about your challenges with trusted individuals can provide perspective and validation.
7. **Practice Self-Compassion:** Be kind and gentle with yourself, especially during difficult times. Treat yourself with the same compassion and understanding that you would offer to a loved one facing similar challenges.

8. **Focus on Solutions:** Instead of dwelling on problems, focus on finding solutions and taking proactive steps to address them. Break down complex issues into manageable tasks and tackle them one at a time.

9. **Embrace Failure as a Learning Opportunity:** Shift your perspective on failure, viewing it as a natural part of the learning process rather than a reflection of your worth. Extract lessons from setbacks and use them to fuel personal growth and resilience.

10. **Practice Gratitude:** Cultivate a gratitude practice to shift your focus from what's lacking to what you're grateful for. Regularly acknowledge and appreciate the positive aspects of your life, no matter how small.

11. **Engage in Self-Care:** Prioritize self-care activities that nourish your body, mind, and soul. This could include exercise, spending time in nature, practicing hobbies, or engaging in activities that bring you joy.

12. **Stay Flexible and Adapt:** Remain flexible and adaptable in the face of challenges, recognizing that setbacks are temporary and opportunities for growth are endless. Embrace change as an inevitable part of life's journey.

By implementing these steps, you can confront the challenges that triumph over your mind with courage, and self-compassion. Remember that you are capable of overcoming adversity and thriving in the face of uncertainty.

NURTURING SELF-GRATITUDE AND APPRECIATION

Gratitude and appreciation of self are essential components of self-care and well-being. Here are some steps to cultivate gratitude and appreciation for oneself:

Practice Self-Reflection: Take time regularly to reflect on your strengths, accomplishments, and positive qualities. Acknowledge the challenges you've overcome and the progress you've made, no matter how small.

1. **Keep a Gratitude Journal:** Dedicate a journal or notebook to write down things you're grateful for, including aspects of yourself that you appreciate. This could range from personal traits to experiences that have shaped you positively.
2. **Celebrate Achievements:** Celebrate your accomplishments, both big and small. Recognize your efforts and successes and give yourself credit for your hard work and determination.
3. **Practice Self-Compassion:** Be kind to yourself, especially in moments of difficulty or failure. Treat yourself with the same compassion and understanding that you would offer to a friend facing similar challenges.
4. **Engage in Self-Care Activities:** Prioritize activities that nurture your physical, emotional, and mental well-being. This could include exercise, meditation, spending time in nature, or engaging in hobbies and interests that bring you joy.
5. **Surround Yourself with Positive Influences:** Surround yourself with people who uplift and support you, and limit exposure to negative influences that undermine your self-worth.
6. **Challenge Negative Self-Talk:** Pay attention to your inner dialogue and challenge negative self-talk. Replace self-criticism with affirmations and positive messages that reinforce your value and worthiness.
7. **Set Boundaries:** Establish healthy boundaries in your relationships and commitments. Prioritize your needs and well-being, and don't hesitate to say no to things that drain your energy or detract from your self-care.
8. **Seek Support:** Don't hesitate to seek support from friends, family, or a therapist if you're struggling to cultivate gratitude and appreciation for yourself. Talking to others can provide perspective and validation.

9. **Practice Mindfulness:** Cultivate mindfulness by being present in the moment and appreciating the beauty and goodness around you. Mindfulness can help you develop a deeper sense of gratitude for yourself and your life.

Remember that cultivating gratitude and appreciation for oneself is an ongoing practice that requires patience and self-compassion. Be gentle with yourself as you embark on this journey of self-discovery and self-love.

May we *continue to embrace our vulnerabilities, lean into discomfort, and cultivate a spirit of resilience in all that we do*. And may we always remember that within each of us lies the power to rise strong—to face our challenges with courage, compassion, and grace, and to emerge from the depths of adversity with newfound strength and resilience. *As we turn the page to the next chapter of our journey, let us do so with open hearts, open minds, and a steadfast commitment to embracing resilience and inner strength in all aspects of our lives.* For it is through the power of rising strong that we discover the true depth of our humanity and the limitless potential that lies within us.

CHAPTER SEVEN

EMBRACING MY BRILLIANCE

In this pivotal chapter of self-discovery and empowerment, we embark on a transformative journey of claiming our power, owning our successes, and embracing the fullness of our achievements. As black women, our narratives are rich with resilience, determination, and the triumph of spirit over adversity. In the pursuit of claiming our power, we dismantle the shackles of societal expectations and redefine what it means to thrive on our own terms.

We begin by acknowledging the multifaceted nature of our successes. Our achievements extend far beyond the boundaries of conventional definitions, encompassing both tangible accomplishments and the intangible growth of our souls. From professional milestones to personal victories, we honor every step of our journey as a testament to our strength and resilience.

As we claim our power, we confront the insidious voices of doubt and insecurity that seek to undermine our confidence. We refuse to internalize the narratives of inadequacy imposed upon us by society, instead embracing the inherent brilliance that radiates from within. With unwavering self-belief, we silence the doubters and step boldly into the fullness of our potential.

Our journey towards claiming our power is not without its challenges. We navigate systemic barriers and confront the pervasive forces of racism, sexism, and intersectional oppression that seek to diminish our worth. Yet, with unwavering determination and solidarity, we rise above adversity and pave the way for future generations to follow.

In reclaiming our power, we celebrate the sisterhood and solidarity of our community. Through mentorship, collaboration, and mutual support, we uplift one another and amplify our collective voices. We recognize that our individual successes are intertwined with the progress of our community, and we commit to lifting as we climb.

As we journey towards self-empowerment, we prioritize self-care, well-being, and balance. We honor the importance of rest, reflection, and rejuvenation in sustaining our inner strength and resilience. By nurturing our minds, bodies, and spirits, we cultivate a foundation of wholeness from which to claim our power and shine brightly.

In the pages that follow, we celebrate the stories of triumph and resilience that define our journey of claiming our power. Through raw and unapologetic narratives, we honor the strength, resilience, and unwavering spirit of black women everywhere. May this chapter serve as a testament to the power that resides within each of us and inspire future generations to boldly claim their place in the world.

Welcome to Chapter 7 of "Embracing My Brilliance" it serves as a reminder that challenges are an inevitable part of life, but they do not define us. As black women, we possess a strength and resilience that is unparalleled, and it is through navigating challenges that we truly embrace our brilliance and shine brightly in the world.

CONFRONT WHAT COMES TO UNDERMINE YOUR CONFIDENCE

Confronting what undermines your confidence can be a challenging but empowering process. Here are steps to help you navigate this journey:

1. **Identify the Undermining Factors:** Take time to identify the specific factors or situations that undermine your confidence. This could include negative self-talk, comparison to others, past failures, criticism from others, or fear of failure. Understanding what triggers your lack of confidence is the first step in addressing it.

2. **Challenge Negative Self-Talk:** Become aware of the negative thoughts and beliefs you have about yourself and challenge them with evidence to the contrary. Practice self-compassion and replace self-critical thoughts with more balanced and affirming ones. Remind yourself of your strengths, accomplishments, and resilience.

3. **Set Realistic Expectations:** Avoid setting unrealistic expectations for yourself, as this can lead to feelings of inadequacy and self-doubt. Break large goals into smaller, achievable steps, and celebrate your progress along the way. Focus on continuous improvement rather than perfection.

4. **Practice Self-Care:** Prioritize self-care activities that nourish your mind, body, and spirit. Engage in activities that bring you joy, relaxation, and fulfillment, whether it's exercise, meditation, spending time with loved ones, or pursuing hobbies. Taking care of yourself strengthens your resilience and confidence.

5. **Seek Support:** Reach out to supportive friends, family members, mentors, or professionals for encouragement and guidance. Surround yourself with people who believe in you and uplift you. Share your struggles and vulnerabilities with trusted individuals who can offer perspective and support.

6. **Develop Coping Strategies:** Develop healthy coping strategies to manage stress, anxiety, and self-doubt when they arise. This could include deep breathing exercises, visualization techniques, positive affirmations, or journaling. Find what works best for you and incorporate it into your daily routine.

7. **Learn from Setbacks:** View setbacks and failures as opportunities for growth and learning rather than reflections of your worth. Analyze what went wrong objectively, identify lessons learned, and use them to inform your future actions. Embrace resilience and perseverance in the face of adversity.

8. **Practice Assertiveness:** Assert yourself confidently in challenging situations, whether it's speaking up for your needs, setting boundaries, or addressing criticism. Use assertive communication techniques such as "I" statements, active listening, and respectful assertiveness to express yourself effectively.

9. **Celebrate Your Successes:** Acknowledge and celebrate your achievements, no matter how small. Keep a success journal to record your accomplishments and milestones and revisit it regularly to boost your confidence. Cultivate a mindset of self-appreciation and gratitude for your progress.

10. **Seek** Professional Help if Needed: If low confidence significantly impacts your daily life or mental well-being, consider seeking support from a therapist or counselor. Professional guidance can help you explore underlying issues, develop coping strategies, and build resilience in confronting what undermines your confidence.

By following these steps and committing to your growth and self-discovery, you can confront what undermines your confidence with courage, resilience, and empowerment. Remember that building confidence is a journey, and each step you take brings you closer to reclaiming your sense of self-worth and living authentically.

CLAIM YOUR POWER

Claiming your power is a deeply personal journey that involves recognizing your worth, embracing your strengths, and asserting yourself confidently in the world. Here are steps to guide you on this empowering journey:

1. **Know Yourself:** Take time to reflect on your values, passions, and strengths. Understanding who you are and what you stand for is essential for claiming your power authentically.
2. **Identify Your Goals:** Clarify what you want to achieve and set clear, actionable goals for yourself. Whether they are related to your career, personal growth, or relationships, having clear goals provides direction and purpose.
3. **Speak Your Truth:** Own your voice and speak up for yourself. Express your thoughts, feelings, and opinions confidently, and advocate for your needs and desires without fear of judgment or rejection.
4. **Take Action:** Take proactive steps towards your goals and aspirations. Break down big goals into smaller, manageable tasks, and consistently take action to move forward. Action breeds confidence and momentum.
5. **Set Boundaries:** Establish healthy boundaries to protect your time, energy, and well-being. Learn to say no to things that do not align with your priorities or values and communicate your boundaries assertively.
6. **Overcome Self-Doubt:** Recognize and challenge the negative self-talk and limiting beliefs that may be holding you back. Cultivate a positive mindset and affirm your worthiness to claim your power.
7. **Embrace Failure:** View failure as a natural part of the learning process and an opportunity for growth. Embrace setbacks as valuable lessons and use them to fuel your resilience and determination.

8. **Practice Self-Compassion:** Be kind to yourself and treat yourself with the same compassion and understanding you would offer to a friend. Accept yourself fully, flaws and all, and forgive yourself for past mistakes.

9. **Surround Yourself with Support**: Cultivate a supportive network of friends, family, mentors, and allies who believe in your potential and encourage your growth. Surrounding yourself with positive influences can uplift and empower you on your journey.

10. **Celebrate Your Achievements:** Acknowledge and celebrate your successes, no matter how small. Take pride in your accomplishments and reflect on how far you've come. Celebrating your achievements boosts your confidence and reinforces your belief in your ability to claim your power.

Remember, claiming your power is an ongoing process that requires self-awareness, courage, and perseverance. Trust in yourself and your abilities, and embrace the journey of becoming the empowered, authentic version of yourself.

As we reflect on our experiences, we have come to realize that our brilliance is not defined by external accolades or accomplishments, but by the unique essence of who we are—our passions, our values, our strengths, and our authentic selves.

We have embraced the power of self-awareness, recognizing the beauty and value of our individuality. We have celebrated our accomplishments and acknowledged our worthiness, refusing to diminish our light for the comfort of others.

In embracing our brilliance, we have shattered the constraints of self-doubt and insecurity, stepping boldly into our power and owning our unique gifts and talents. We have embraced the fullness of who we are, unapologetically expressing ourselves and sharing our light with the world.

But our journey does not end here—it is an ongoing quest for growth, learning, and self-discovery. As we continue on our path, let us carry with us the lessons we have learned and the wisdom we have gained. Let us continue to embrace our brilliance with humility, gratitude, and a sense of awe at the infinite potential within us.

May we never forget the power of our own brilliance—the power to inspire, to create, to transform, and to shine brightly in the world. And may we always remember that our brilliance is not just something we possess—it is who we are, at our very core.

In the chapters that follow, may we continue to embrace our brilliance with courage, grace, and unwavering confidence. For it is in embracing our brilliance that we find the true essence of who we are and the boundless potential of what we can become.

CHAPTER EIGHT

THE JOURNEY AHEAD: CONTINUING TO GROW AND THRIVE

As we stand on the threshold of the future, we are filled with anticipation, excitement, and a profound sense of purpose. Chapter 8 marks not the end of our journey, but the beginning of a new chapter—a chapter brimming with endless possibilities, opportunities for growth, and the promise of continued transformation.

In the chapters that have unfolded thus far, we have journeyed deep within ourselves, confronted our fears, and embraced our power with courage and determination. We have celebrated our successes, learned from our failures, and emerged stronger and more resilient than ever before. But our journey is far from over—it is an ongoing quest for self-discovery, fulfillment, and meaning.

As we look to the journey ahead, we do so with a sense of optimism and excitement. We know that there will be challenges to face, obstacles to overcome, and lessons to learn along the way. But we also know that with each challenge comes an opportunity for growth, and with each lesson comes a chance to become wiser and more resilient.

In the journey ahead, we will continue to push ourselves beyond our comfort zones, daring to dream bigger, reach higher, and aim for the stars. We will embrace change as a catalyst for growth and transformation, knowing that it is through embracing the unknown that we find the greatest opportunities for personal and professional development. We will remain steadfast in our commitment to authenticity, integrity, and self-love, knowing that these are the pillars upon which we build our brightest future. We will honor our values, follow our passions, and stay true to ourselves, even in the face of adversity.

Along the way, we will lean on our *support systems—our friends, families, mentors, and allies—for guidance, encouragement, and inspiration.* We will lift each other up, celebrate each other's successes, and offer a helping hand to those in need. For we know that we are stronger together, and that by supporting each other, we all rise.

As we continue our journey, we will remain open to the possibilities that lie ahead, trusting in the wisdom of the universe and the guidance of our own intuition. We will embrace uncertainty with courage and grace, knowing that it is through embracing the unknown that we find the greatest opportunities for growth and discovery.

And as *we move forward, we will never forget the lessons we have learned along the way—the moments of triumph*, the moments of struggle, and everything in between. For it is these experiences that have shaped us into the resilient, compassionate, and empowered individuals we are today.

So let us embark on the journey ahead with open hearts and open minds, ready to embrace whatever may come our way. For we know that the road ahead may be long and winding, but with courage, determination, and a fierce belief in ourselves, we will continue to grow, thrive, and shine brightly in the world.

EMBRACED YOUR POWER

Embracing your power is a journey of self-discovery, self-awareness, and self-empowerment. Here are steps to guide you on this transformative journey:

1. **Know Yourself:** Take time to explore and understand yourself on a deeper level. Reflect on your values, strengths, passions, and aspirations. Understanding who you are and what you stand for is essential for embracing your power authentically.
2. **Acknowledge Your Worth:** Recognize your inherent worthiness and value as a unique individual. Let go of self-doubt, comparison, and negative self-talk. Embrace self-acceptance and cultivate a positive self-image rooted in self-love and self-respect.
3. **Identify Your Strengths:** Celebrate your strengths, talents, and abilities. Acknowledge the qualities that make you unique and special. Lean into your strengths and leverage them to pursue your goals and aspirations with confidence and conviction.
4. **Set Clear Intentions:** Define what it means to you to embrace your power. Set clear intentions for how you want to show up in the world and the impact you want to make. Visualize yourself embodying your power and living your life authentically and boldly.
5. **Set Clear Intentions:** Define what it means to you to embrace your power. Set clear intentions for how you want to show up in the world and the impact you want to make. Visualize yourself embodying your power and living your life authentically and boldly.
6. **Own Your Voice:** Speak up for yourself and express your thoughts, opinions, and desires with confidence and assertiveness. Advocate for your needs and boundaries and assert yourself in situations where your voice may be overlooked or silenced.
7. **Practice Self-Compassion:** Be kind and gentle with yourself as you navigate your journey of self-empowerment. Treat yourself with the same compassion and understanding you would offer to a friend. Embrace imperfection and forgive yourself for past mistakes or setbacks.

8. **Surround Yourself with Support:** Surround yourself with people who uplift, encourage, and support you on your journey. Seek out mentors, friends, and allies who believe in your potential and inspire you to be your best self. Connect with communities and networks that resonate with your values and aspirations.

9. **Take Inspired Action:** Take intentional action towards embracing your power and living in alignment with your values and purpose. Set goals, create action plans, and take consistent steps towards manifesting your vision for yourself and your life.

10. **Celebrate Your Growth:** Acknowledge and celebrate your progress and growth along the way. Celebrate your achievements, no matter how small, and recognize the courage and resilience it takes to embrace your power authentically. Reflect on how far you've come and honor the journey you've traveled.

Remember, embracing your power is an ongoing process that requires courage, self-awareness, and commitment. Trust in yourself, believe in your potential, and embrace the journey of becoming the empowered, authentic version of yourself you are meant to be.

DR LOVELLA MOGERE

CHAPTER NINE

THE ESSENCE OF YOU, BLACK WOMAN

In this chapter, we delve into the essence of what it means to be a Black woman—a journey of self-discovery, resilience, and celebration of our unique identity. We explore the multifaceted layers of our being, each one adding depth and richness to the tapestry of our existence.

As Black women, we carry within us the legacy of our ancestors—their strength, wisdom, and resilience coursing through our veins. We are the embodiment of centuries of triumphs and struggles, victories and setbacks, resilience, and resistance. Our stories are woven into the fabric of history, shaping the world in profound and enduring ways.

At the core of our essence lies our unapologetic authenticity—the unwavering commitment to be true to ourselves and honor our lived experiences. We refuse to conform to society's narrow expectations or limitations, boldly asserting our right to exist and thrive on our own terms.

Our essence is rooted in our—the ability to rise above adversity, overcome obstacles, and persevere in the face of adversity. We carry within us the indomitable spirit of our foremothers, who faced unimaginable challenges with grace, dignity, and strength.

We are the embodiment of beauty in all its forms—our melanin-rich skin glowing with radiance, our features sculpted by centuries of ancestry and heritage. We embrace our natural hair, our curves, our imperfections, knowing that true beauty lies in embracing our uniqueness and celebrating our authentic selves.

Our essence is defined by our sisterhood—the bonds of solidarity and kinship that unite us as a community. We uplift and support one another, sharing our joys and sorrows, triumphs, and tribulations. In each other, we find strength, inspiration, and empowerment.

As Black women, we are the architects of our own destiny—the authors of our own stories, the creators of our own reality. We refuse to be confined by the limitations imposed upon us by society, reclaiming our power and agency to shape a future that reflects our hopes, dreams, and aspirations.

In the essence of you, Black woman, lies the promise of endless possibilities—the potential to transcend boundaries, defy expectations, and leave an indelible mark on the world. Embrace your essence wholeheartedly, knowing that you are worthy, you are powerful, and you are enough, just as you are.

WE ARE THE ARCHITECTS OF OUR OWN DESTINY

Black women are indeed the architects of our own destiny, empowered by our resilience, strength, and unwavering determination to shape our lives according to our own vision and aspirations. Here's how:

1. **Self-Determination:** Black women possess an innate sense of self-determination and agency, refusing to be confined by societal expectations or limitations. We recognize that our destinies are ours to create, and we boldly take ownership of our lives, making choices that align with our values, goals, and dreams.
2. **Empowerment Through Education:** Despite historical barriers to education, Black women have pursued knowledge and learning with fervor, equipping themselves with the tools and skills needed to carve out

their own paths. Education empowers us to challenge stereotypes, break down barriers, and pursue opportunities that were once denied to us.

3. **Entrepreneurship and Innovation:** Black women are trailblazers in entrepreneurship and innovation, founding businesses, creating wealth, and driving economic growth in our communities. We harness our creativity, resilience, and resourcefulness to build thriving enterprises that reflect our unique talents and visions.

4. **Leadership and Advocacy:** Black women are at the forefront of movements for social justice, equality, and change, using our voices and platforms to advocate for the rights and dignity of all people. We lead by example, mobilizing communities, influencing policies, and effecting positive transformation in society.

5. **Cultural Influence and Creativity:** Black women have made significant contributions to art, literature, music, fashion, and culture, shaping the cultural landscape, and leaving an indelible mark on history. Our creativity, innovation, and artistic expression inspire and uplift others, challenging stereotypes and amplifying marginalized voices.

6. **Resilience and Perseverance:** Despite facing systemic oppression, discrimination, and adversity, Black women have demonstrated unparalleled resilience and perseverance. We draw strength from our ancestors, who endured unimaginable hardships with grace and dignity, and we carry their legacy forward with pride and determination.

7. **Resilience and Perseverance:** Despite facing systemic oppression, discrimination, and adversity, Black women have demonstrated unparalleled resilience and perseverance. We draw strength from our ancestors, who endured unimaginable hardships with grace and dignity, and we carry their legacy forward with pride and determination.

In every aspect of life, Black women are the architects of our own destiny, empowered by our resilience, strength, and unwavering belief in our ability to create positive change. We continue to defy expectations, break down barriers, and pave the way for future generations to thrive.

BLACK WOMEN CARRY WITHIN THEM THE LEGACY OF OUR ANCESTORS

Black women carry within them the legacy of our ancestors in profound and multifaceted ways, embodying their strength, resilience, wisdom, and indomitable spirit. Here's how:

1. **Resilience:** Throughout history, Black women have faced unimaginable hardships, including slavery, colonization, oppression, and systemic racism. Despite these challenges, our ancestors exhibited remarkable resilience, enduring unspeakable atrocities with courage and perseverance. Black women today carry on this legacy of resilience, drawing strength from the struggles and triumphs of those who came before us.

2. **Strength:** Our ancestors, particularly Black women, were pillars of strength within their communities, holding families together, providing support, and nurturing future generations. They bore the weight of systemic oppression and racial violence with grace and dignity, inspiring us to stand tall in the face of adversity and to confront injustice with courage and resolve.

3. **Wisdom:** Black women have long been the keepers of ancestral knowledge, passing down traditions, stories, and cultural practices from generation to generation. Our ancestors imparted invaluable wisdom about survival, resilience, and resistance, teaching us to honor our heritage, embrace our identity, and navigate the complexities of life with wisdom and grace.

4. **Spirituality:** African spirituality and traditions have played a central role in the lives of Black women throughout history, providing solace, guidance, and a sense of connection to our ancestors and the divine. Our spiritual practices are deeply rooted in the wisdom and teachings of our foremothers, who revered the earth, honored the

ancestors, and sought healing and empowerment through ritual and ceremony.

5. **Activism and Advocacy:** Black women have been at the forefront of movements for social justice, equality, and liberation, continuing the legacy of our ancestors who fought tirelessly for freedom and dignity. From Harriet Tubman and Sojourner Truth to Fannie Lou Hamer and Audre Lorde, Black women activists have paved the way for progress, using their voices and platforms to challenge oppression and uplift marginalized communities.

6. **Cultural Heritage**: Black women carry within them the rich cultural heritage and traditions passed down by our ancestors, from music, art, and literature to cuisine, dance, and fashion. Our cultural legacy is a source of pride and identity, connecting us to our roots and reminding us of the resilience, creativity, and ingenuity of our ancestors.

In every aspect of our lives, Black women carry within us the legacy of our ancestors—a legacy of strength, resilience, wisdom, and empowerment that inspires us to honor our heritage, embrace our identity, and continue the fight for justice and equality.

In "The Essence of You, Black Woman," we are reminded of the profound beauty, strength, and resilience that defines the essence of Black women. Throughout this chapter, we have explored the multifaceted layers of our being, celebrating the richness of our identity, heritage, and lived experiences.

We have embraced our authenticity, refusing to be confined by society's narrow expectations or limitations. Instead, we boldly assert our right to exist and thrive on our own terms, embracing our natural beauty, celebrating our uniqueness, and honoring our heritage with pride and reverence.

THE CONFESSIONS OF A BLACK WOMAN

The essence of Black women is rooted in resilience—the ability to rise above adversity, overcome obstacles, and persevere in the face of challenges. We carry within us the indomitable spirit of our ancestors, drawing strength from their struggles and triumphs as we navigate the complexities of existence with grace and determination.

Our sisterhood is a source of strength and empowerment, uniting us in solidarity and kinship as we support and uplift one another. Together, we stand as a testament to the power of unity, resilience, and collective action, inspiring positive change, and transformation in our communities and beyond.

As we continue our journey of self-discovery and empowerment, let us embrace the essence of who we are as Black women—bold, resilient, and unapologetically authentic. May we honor our heritage, celebrate our uniqueness, and continue to shine brightly as we embrace our true selves and shape our destinies with courage, grace, and unwavering determination.

DR LOVELLA MOGERE

CHAPTER TEN

HONORING THE FORTITUDE OF THE BLACK WOMEN

In this chapter, we pay tribute to the unparalleled fortitude of Black women—a strength that has sustained us through adversity, empowered us to rise above challenges, and inspired us to create positive change in our communities and beyond.

The fortitude of Black women is rooted in the ability to bounce back from setbacks, overcome obstacles, and thrive in the face of adversity. From the struggles of our ancestors to the present day, Black women have demonstrated an unwavering resolve to persevere, no matter the odds.

We honor the fortitude of Black women in the countless ways we show up for ourselves, our families, and our communities. Despite facing systemic oppression, discrimination, and marginalization, we continue to rise with grace and dignity, refusing to be defined by the limitations imposed upon us.

Our fortitude is evident in our leadership—whether in the boardroom, the classroom, or the streets. Black women have been at the forefront of movements for social justice, equality, and liberation, using our voices and platforms to advocate for change and challenge injustice.

We honor the fortitude of Black women in our commitment to uplifting and supporting one another. In the face of adversity, we come together as sisters, offering solace, strength, and solidarity. We recognize the power of sisterhood in healing, resilience, and collective empowerment.

THE CONFESSIONS OF A BLACK WOMAN

The fortitude of Black women is reflected in our creativity, innovation, and resilience. From art and literature to music and fashion, Black women have made indelible contributions to culture and society, shaping the cultural landscape, and leaving a legacy for generations to come.

As we honor the fortitude of Black women, let us also acknowledge the importance of self-care and self-compassion. We must prioritize our well-being, nurture our spirits, and seek support when needed. For it is through caring for ourselves that we replenish our strength and continue to shine brightly in the world.

In honoring the fortitude of Black women, we celebrate our resilience, our strength, and our unwavering commitment to creating a better world for ourselves and future generations. May we continue to draw inspiration from the courage of those who came before us, and may we carry their spirit forward with pride, dignity, and unwavering resolve.

In the journey of honoring the fortitude of Black women is an ongoing testament to resilience, strength, and unwavering determination. Throughout this chapter, we have celebrated the indomitable spirit that has defined Black women throughout history and continues to shape our lives today.

As we reflect on the countless ways in which Black women have demonstrated fortitude—in the face of adversity, discrimination, and injustice—we are reminded of the power of resilience to overcome even the greatest of challenges. From the struggles of our ancestors to the present day, Black women have stood tall with grace and dignity, refusing to be broken by the burdens we carry.

In honoring the fortitude of Black women, we also acknowledge the importance of self-care, self-compassion, and community support. We recognize that fortitude does not mean bearing our burdens alone but rather finding strength in our connections with one another and in our commitment to uplifting and empowering one another.

As we continue our journey, let us carry forward the legacy of fortitude passed down to us by our ancestors, inspiring future generations to stand strong in the face of adversity and to never lose sight of the power within themselves.

May we honor the fortitude of Black women with gratitude, reverence, and a deep sense of pride, knowing that our resilience, strength, and unwavering determination are the foundations upon which we build a brighter future for ourselves and for generations to come.

CHAPTER ELEVEN

BLACK WOMAN, YOU ARE ENOUGH

To the Black Women,

As we conclude this journey together, I want to leave you with a few final words of encouragement, empowerment, and affirmation.

You are enough. You are worthy. You are powerful beyond measure.

In a world that often seeks to diminish your light, remember that you shine with a brilliance that cannot be dimmed. Your resilience, your strength, your fortitude—they are the pillars upon which our communities stand, the bedrock of our collective strength.

Embrace your authenticity. Own your truth. Your voice matters, your story matters, and your presence in this world makes a difference.

You are not alone. You are surrounded by a sisterhood of Black women who stand with you, support you, and uplift you. Lean on each other, celebrate with each other, and continue to show up for one another with love and solidarity.

As you navigate the complexities of life, remember to prioritize your well-being. Take time to care for yourself, to nurture your spirit, and to replenish your strength. Your health, your happiness, and your peace of mind are invaluable treasures that deserve to be cherished and protected.

Never forget the power that resides within you. You are the architects of your own destiny, the creators of your own reality. Believe in your dreams, pursue your passions, and trust in your ability to overcome any obstacle that stands in your way.

And above all, know that you are loved. You are valued. You are seen. Thank you for sharing your stories, your struggles, and your triumphs. Your courage and resilience inspire us all, and your journey of self-discovery and empowerment will continue to ripple out into the world, touching hearts and transforming lives.

Keep shining, keep striving, and keep embracing the beautiful essence of who you are—unapologetically, authentically, and fearlessly.

With love and solidarity,

Dr Lovella Mogere

Made in the USA
Monee, IL
18 October 2024